WILDLIFE
AT RISK

MONKEYS

Tess Lemmon

WILDLIFE AT RISK

Bears
Birds of Prey
Elephants
Gorillas
Monkeys
Pandas
Rhinos
Seals and Sea Lions
Tigers
Whales and Dolphins

Book editor: Cally Chambers
Series designer: Marilyn Clay

Cover: Although the squirrel monkey is
not a rare species, it is still important to
protect its habitat for the future.

First published in 1991 by
Wayland (Publishers) Ltd
61 Western Road, Hove
East Sussex BN3 1JD, England

**British Library Cataloguing in
Publication Data**
Lemmon, Tess
    Monkeys.
    1. Monkeys
    I. Title II. Series
    599.82

    ISBN 0-7502-0030-8

Typeset by Dorchester Typesetting Group Ltd.
Printed and bound in Italy by L.E.G.O. S.p.A.

Contents

All words printed in **bold** are explained in the glossary on page 30.

WHAT ARE MONKEYS AND APES?

There are 133 different kinds of monkey and most of them are about the same size as a pet cat, but some are much smaller. The smallest monkey weighs only 125 g and can fit into the palm of a hand. It is called the pygmy marmoset.

The mandrill is one of the biggest monkeys. It is 80 cm long, and weighs 400 times more than the tiny pygmy marmoset. Mandrills have bright red and blue faces. Some other monkeys have long fringes, beards, manes or moustaches.

Above *The emperor tamarin has a long moustache and a beard.*

Left *The pygmy marmoset is so small that it can cling to a blade of grass.*

Most monkeys have short noses, but the proboscis monkey is different. Proboscis is another word for nose.

When you first look at monkeys they seem quite different from each other, but really they are very alike. Most monkeys live in trees, and they have certain features which make it easy for them to live high above the ground.

All monkeys have very good eyesight. Their eyes are at the front of their faces, not at the side like many animals. This means that monkeys can look at what is ahead of them as they jump and swing through the trees. Many animals see only in black and white, but monkeys can see in colour. Because their eyesight is good, monkeys use their eyes more than their noses. So usually they have short noses and their sense of smell is not very good.

Monkeys use their hands and feet to get about. They have long fingers and toes to grip on to branches of trees and some monkeys even have thumbs on their feet.

Left The chimpanzee is an ape, not a monkey. Apes do not have tails.

Below The spider monkey holds on to a branch with its strong tail. The baby wraps its tail round its mother's and rides on her back.

Monkeys are closely related to apes. Chimpanzees, gorillas, orang-utans and gibbons are all apes. Monkeys and apes belong to a group of animals called **primates**. Human beings are also primates and our closest 'relatives' are chimpanzees.

Monkeys and apes are very similar but all apes, except gibbons, are bigger than monkeys. The biggest ape is the gorilla and an adult male weighs more than two men.

Apes do not have tails. This is the easiest way to tell an ape from a monkey. All monkeys have tails, even though some are only short ones. Some monkeys have a bare patch at the end of their tail which is just like the palm of a hand. It works like another hand, and holds on to branches as the monkey climbs through the trees.

Monkeys are divided into two main groups according to which part of the world they live in. New World monkeys live in Central and South America. Old World monkeys live in Africa and Asia.

Monkeys belong to a group of animals called mammals. Mammals are usually furry or hairy and they feed their babies with milk. Mammals have warm blood, which means in hot or cold weather they keep their bodies at the same temperature.

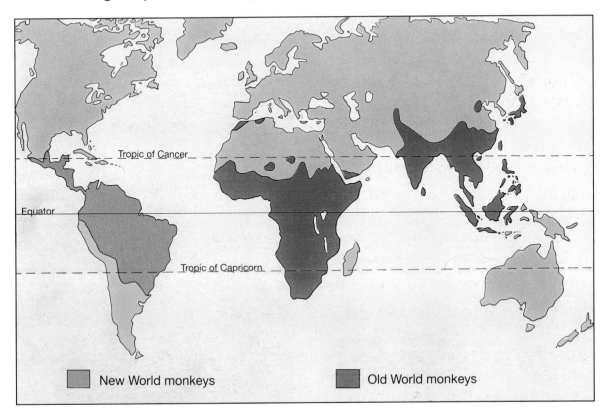

Tropic of Cancer

Equator

Tropic of Capricorn

New World monkeys   Old World monkeys

THE FOREST HOME

Monkeys live in hot countries where it rains a lot. The sun and the rain help to make the forests grow thick and tall. Most monkeys are to be found in these **tropical** forests.

Monkeys often live in trees that are as tall as buildings. Some of them hardly ever come down to the ground. They find their way around by using pathways through the branches, just as if they were following paths on the ground.

The trees provide the monkeys with everything they need. The branches provide comfortable places to sleep.

The world's tropical rainforests

● Now cover 6 per cent of the Earth's surface.

● Are home to almost half of the wild animals, plants, birds and insects known on Earth – at least 3 to 5 million **species**.

● Have trees up to 50 m high.

Monkeys use their hands to hold things. This macaque is eating a flower.

The leaves shelter the monkeys from the sun and the rain, and hide them from **predators** such as leopards and snakes. There is plenty of food up in the trees and the monkeys eat fruit, flowers, seeds and leaves. Some monkeys eat a little meat and catch insects and birds from the trees.

Left A vervet monkey stands upright to see better. It is looking out for snakes and leopards.

Below The douroucouli is the only monkey that sleeps in the day and comes out at night. It is also known as the owl monkey.

Baboons, vervet monkeys and patas monkeys are different because they often come down to the ground and feed on grass and seeds. They go up into trees to pick fruit and to sleep. On the ground they sometimes get chased by jackals and other predators. Patas monkeys can run so fast that they are nicknamed greyhounds.

LIVING TOGETHER

All monkeys live together in groups made up of adults and young. The largest of these groups contain many hundreds of animals, but most have between ten and twenty in them. All the members of the group help each other. A monkey that spots a predator warns the others by giving a cry of **alarm** and one that finds a lot of food calls to let the others know.

Monkeys are very good mothers and fathers. Females usually have one baby at a time. The newborn baby clings to the fur on its mother's chest all the time and when it is older it rides on her back. Some fathers carry babies too. In the group, the baby has many relatives. Its grandparents, aunts, uncles, and older brothers and sisters all help to look after it.

These young baboons are playing. The watching adult will stop them if they get too rough. Play is important in group behaviour.

A baby mandrill feeds from its mother. All monkeys take very good care of their children.

Monkeys are not grown-up until they are several years old. They have a long childhood because they have a lot to learn, such as which foods are safe to eat.

They also learn how to behave correctly so they will become adults that fit into the group. Youngsters learn mostly by watching older monkeys in their group.

THE FORESTS ARE DISAPPEARING

The disappearing rainforests

- At least 40 per cent of the world's rainforests have been lost in the last thirty years.

- More than half of the rainforests that stood in 1900 have since been destroyed.

- It is thought that one wildlife species is becoming extinct every day.

- It is thought that an area of rainforest about the size of Britain is cut down each year. This means that about 40 sq km is lost every minute.

Clearing and burning the rainforests leaves monkeys with nowhere to live.

Millions of monkeys die every year because the trees they live in are destroyed.

So many monkeys have died that there are only very small numbers of some species left in the world. These species are in danger of becoming **extinct**. Nearly forty species of monkey are at risk of extinction.

People have always cut down trees for wood. For hundreds of years wood has been used to build with and to make fires. In the past, it took a lot of hard work to chop down just one tree, and so there were enough left for the monkeys to live in. Nowadays, modern machines wipe out a whole forest in a short time.

Often the wood is not really needed. It is bought by richer countries such as the USA, the United Kingdom and Japan, and used to make furniture and even toilet seats.

Trees are not destroyed just for their wood. They are also cleared to make way for farmland, houses and roads. The growing numbers of people in the world seem to need more and more space. But the more room they take up, the less there is left for the monkeys and other animals.

Right *The golden monkey lives only in the cold mountain forests of China.*

Below *The disappearing Amazon rainforest of South America is the home of the uakari.*

One of the rarest monkeys in the world is the woolly spider monkey, or muriqui. There are only about 300 muriquis left in the world. They all live in one forest, called the Atlantic Forest, in Brazil, South America. Most of that forest has been destroyed, but there is now a big **campaign** to save what is left. The muriquis are becoming very famous all over the world because their pictures are on T-shirts, stickers and posters, and they have even had a special film made about them.

Above *Designs showing the muriqui have been used in the campaign to save them and other Brazilian species.*

Left *Many people in Brazil are keen to save the threatened muriqui.*

The golden lion tamarin is named after its mane. It nearly became extinct, but there is now a world-wide project to save it.

In the same forest lives a species of monkey called the golden lion tamarin. Like the muriqui, it does not live anywhere else. When so much of the forest was destroyed, the tamarins nearly became extinct. The only hope left for them was to try to breed them in **captivity**. This was very successful, and now tamarins born in captivity are being put back into the forest.

The Atlantic rainforest in Brazil

● Has only 2 per cent of the original forest still standing.

● Is home to 21 species of monkey, 16 of which are found nowhere else.

● Of these monkeys, 6 species are near to extinction and 14 are in danger.

PEOPLE KILL MONKEYS

Food for people is now grown in many places where monkeys have always lived. Sometimes monkeys come along and help themselves to the corn and other crops in the fields. These raiders are very unpopular with farmers and many of them are shot.

One kind of monkey which is killed for crop-raiding is the hamadryas baboon. It lives in one small part of northern Africa and used to be worshipped as a god by the people who lived in Egypt a long time ago. Now these baboons are thought of as 'vermin' like rats and mice.

The ancient Egyptians used to worship the hamadryas baboon and included it in their religious wall paintings.

Some people are trying to find ways of scaring the baboons away from the fields instead of killing them. One idea is to play them tape recordings of their own alarm calls. This makes them think another baboon is telling them to keep away because a predator is nearby.

When people go to war they kill animals as well as each other. The douc is a species of monkey which is now very **rare** because it lives in Vietnam where there was a war from 1965 to 1975.

Some soldiers shot the monkeys just for fun, but most monkeys died when **chemical poisons** were sprayed over the forests to stop people hiding in them.

Above Hamadryas baboons live in the dry, rocky lands of northern Africa. They search for grass and roots, and steal the farmers' crops.

Right The douc spends a lot of time resting, but it can leap through the trees at great speed.

This drill is one of the largest and rarest kinds of monkey.

The meat most of us eat comes from specially-kept animals such as sheep and pigs. Not everyone in the world keeps animals to eat. Instead, some people go out and hunt wild animals, including monkeys. People have hunted monkeys for hundreds of years and in the past it has not put any species of monkey at risk. However, today some monkeys are hunted in forests which are being destroyed. If the numbers of monkeys are already dropping because their homes are disappearing, then hunting only makes the risk of extinction worse.

One very rare species of monkey, called the drill, lives only in the forests of Cameroon in Africa. Yet the drill's forest **habitat** is still being cut down and it is still hunted for food. Drills are easy to kill because they move around in large, noisy groups, but there is only one place where they are protected from hunters.

Some monkeys are hunted for their skins. People use monkey skins as floor rugs, or hang them on the wall for decoration. Sometimes skins are made into hats. Many people who buy these things are **tourists**. Today, fewer skins are on sale because most people think that monkeys should not be killed and made into souvenirs.

This man in South America is using the tail of a monkey as a duster.

MONKEYS IN CAPTIVITY

Some monkeys are captured alive and sold as pets. Most of these monkeys are babies. Their mothers are killed first and when they fall to the ground the babies are taken away. Many babies die within days of being caught. Some are sold in local markets, but many are **exported** to other countries where people pay a lot of money for them.

This macaque has just been caught in the wild from the forests of Borneo, South East Asia. It will probably be sold and kept as a pet.

Monkeys are not like dogs and cats. They are wild animals and need to live in the wild with other monkeys. Many people have stopped keeping monkeys as pets because they realize it is cruel.

People used to go and capture any animal they wanted. This is how zoos collected their animals. Now there are laws against taking monkeys and other animals

Above Some zoos still keep monkeys in very bad conditions. In these cases, unhappy captive monkeys are likely to die younger.

from the wild. Some people break the law and **smuggle** monkeys from one country to another. Luckily they do not always get away with it and some are caught and punished.

To find out how our bodies work, scientists carry out **experiments** on animals. Many monkeys are used in experiments. They are kept in cages in laboratories and given diseases to make them ill. They are also given **drugs** to see what happens to them. Often the monkeys suffer pain and then die.

Some people say that monkeys must be used in experiments because their bodies are so like ours. Other people think it is not right to make monkeys suffer just

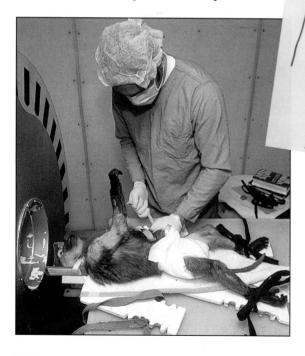

to ... human beings. Some ... f these people ... s of doing ... thout using ... ther animals, ... computers and testing human **cells**.

This is a SAD page boohoo

Left Many monkeys are kept in laboratories and used in experiments. This one is being tied down so it cannot move during the experiment.

Families of long-tailed macaques live near rivers and coasts in South East Asia. They are also known as crab-eating macaques.

Thousands of monkeys are caught in the wild and sent to richer countries to be used in experiments. At one time India exported more than 200,000 rhesus monkeys every year. People got so worried that there would be none left in the wild that the Indian government passed a law to stop any more monkeys being exported. This **ban** saved the rhesus monkeys, but scientists soon found another species of monkey to use. Now thousands of long-tailed macaques are caught in Indonesia and sent to laboratories.

PROTECTING MONKEYS

All over the world there are people helping to save monkeys. One way to save monkeys is to protect the places where they live. Many people are trying to **conserve** the rainforests. By conserving a rainforest they can save all the plants and animals that live there.

We can all help to save the forests. Some of the trees, especially the tropical **hardwoods**, are cut down to make wooden things for us to buy. If we stop buying these things we will save the trees. Some conservation groups are asking shops not to sell goods made from tropical hardwoods. They can be made from other types of wood which do not result in the destruction of the forests.

This guitar and speaker are made from mahogany. If people stop buying hardwood products like these, it will help stop the destruction of the rainforests.

At the Tiwai Island Wildlife Sanctuary, people can learn about monkeys and their habitat, and see them in the wild.

Some forests are protected by law and have been turned into national parks or **sanctuaries**. People can visit them, watch the animals, and learn about the importance of conserving them.

One place like this is the Tiwai Island Wildlife Sanctuary in Sierra Leone, Africa. It is home to eight different species of monkey, as well as chimpanzees. Visitors to the sanctuary can find out about the animals by talking to people who study them. They also get a chance to see some of the animals by following special nature trails through the forest.

A different kind of sanctuary is not in the tropical forest, but in Cornwall, England, where some rare woolly monkeys have been given a home. Woolly monkeys are at risk because their forests in South America are being destroyed.

In zoos woolly monkeys usually die when they are very young because they are kept on their own with nothing to do. At the sanctuary, the monkeys have lots of space and plenty of ropes and trees to climb around on. Also the twenty monkeys all live together as they would in the forest. Some of the monkeys from England are being put back into the wild in a protected part of the forest.

At the Monkey Sanctuary in Cornwall, the monkeys are free to climb up the tree tower and along the ropes to get into the trees.

Many babies are born at the Monkey Sanctuary. This is a three-month-old baby woolly monkey. Its mother was born there too.

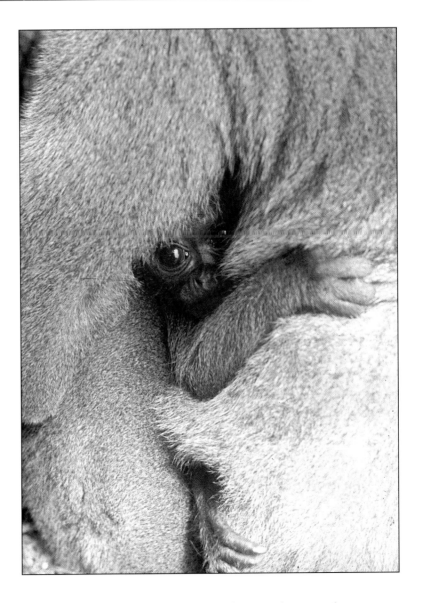

Another way of helping monkeys is to stop people capturing them to sell. Many countries have passed laws to ban the capture of monkeys. Also, many countries sign agreements promising not to buy and sell monkeys that are at risk.

Everyone can help save monkeys by not buying souvenirs that are made out of monkey skin, and by not buying monkeys as pets.

THE FUTURE FOR MONKEYS

The more wildlife workers learn about monkeys and apes, the more they discover what gentle, intelligent creatures they are. But even so, some people do not treat their wildlife relatives very well. They dress them up in clothes and make them do silly tricks, or keep them on their own in bare zoo cages.

Even though a lot of people have changed their ideas about monkeys, many of them

Dressing monkeys in clothes and making them do tricks is becoming a thing of the past.

Dr McGreal runs a rescue home for gibbons. This one was kept in a laboratory for twenty years. His name is Igor.

are still being treated badly. One woman who works to protect monkeys and apes is called Dr Shirley McGreal. Once, when she was at an airport, she saw baby monkeys stacked in crates ready to be sent to a laboratory. When she found there was no one willing to help the monkeys, Dr McGreal set up an **organization** called the International Primate Protection League (IPPL).

The IPPL now helps monkeys and apes all over the world. It helps to protect the ones living in the wild as well as those that have been treated cruelly in captivity.

Perhaps it should not be left just to organizations like the IPPL to look after monkeys and apes. By helping to save

__Above__ The number of rhesus monkeys increased when the Indian government banned its export for use in experiments.

these animals and their rainforest habitats we can all make sure that monkeys and apes will continue to share the Earth with us.

Glossary

Alarm   A warning of danger.

Ban   To make against the law.

Campaign   Working together to persuade people.

Captivity   Kept in a place that is not a natural habitat.

Cells   The tiny parts that make up most living things.

Chemical poisons   Substances which can kill living things.

Conserve   To protect now and for the future.

Drugs   Substances which people take to alter the way their bodies work. Medicines are drugs, but so are some substances which do harm.

Experiments   Tests to find out how something works.

Exported   Sent out of one country to another.

Extinct   When a species has died out completely.

Habitat   The place where an animal or plant naturally lives.

Hardwoods   Wood, such as mahogany, which is useful for making things because it is very solid. Hardwoods take a long time to grow.

Organization   A group of people working together.

Predators   Animals that kill and eat other animals.

Primates   The name of a group of animals to which monkeys, apes and humans belong.

Rare   When only a few are left.

Sanctuaries   Places where animals and plants are protected.

Smuggle   To take something secretly into or out of a country.

Species   Living things which are alike and able to produce young with each other.

Tourists   People who go sight-seeing on holiday.

Tropical   In the hot parts of the world near the Equator.

Picture acknowledgements

The publishers would like to thank the following: BBC Wildlife 24 (Julian Monahan); Biofotos 8; Bruce Coleman Ltd. 20 (Bingham), 9 above (Burton), *cover* (Crichton), 4 below (Freeman), 17 left (Futil), 4 above (Marigo), 11 (Overcash), 6 above (Reinhard), 23 (Taylor), 5, 9 below, 15, 17 right (Williams); Frank Lane Picture Agency 28 above (Henry), 29 (Lawrence), 13 right (Nostrand), 6 below (Wothe); Frank Spooner Pictures 22; Kate Hill 25; IPPL 28 below; R. A. Mittermeier 14 below, 19; The Monkey Sanctuary 26, 27; Stephen Nash 14 above; Oxford Scientific Films 13 inset (Clare), 12 (Morris), 18 (Leszczynski); Survival Anglia 10 (Borland); Zefa 16 (Scholz); Zoo Check 21. The map on page 7 is by John Yates.

Further reading

The books listed below may help you to find out more about monkeys, their habitat and other wildlife at risk.

Conserving Rainforests Martin Banks (Wayland, 1989)
Endangered Animals Malcolm Penny (Wayland, 1988)
Monkey Mary Hoffman (Methuen, 1985)
Monkeys and Apes Norman Barrett (Franklin Watts, 1988)

Monkeys and Apes Sarah Matthews (Longman, 1985)
Protecting Wildlife Malcolm Penny (Wayland, 1989)
Tropical Rainforest Michael Bright (Aladdin, 1991)

Useful addresses

If you would like to help conserve monkeys and other wildlife at risk, or find out more information, contact the organizations listed below.

Fauna and Flora Preservation Society
79-83 North Street
Brighton
East Sussex BN1 1ZA

Friends of the Earth (UK)
26-28 Underwood Street
London N1 7JQ

World Wide Fund for Nature (UK)
Panda House
Weyside Park
Catteshall Lane
Godalming
Surrey GU7 1XR

International Primate Protection League (UK)
116 Judd Street
London WC1H 9NS

International Primate Protection League (USA)
PO Box 766
Summerville
SC 29484
USA

Conservation International
1015 18 Street NW
Washington DC 20036
USA

Index